Praise for Jared Smith:

"The whims of literary recognition are inscrutable. If they were logical or fair, Jared Smith would be renowned as one of America's most prodigious poets. Though it might be tempting to draw comparisons to W.S. Merwin, Jack Gilbert, or Galway Kinnell, Smith is unmistakably his own poet—and he has been for five decades. His topics range from civil rights to transcendentalism to ecopsychology, all of which he has experienced and embodied. As a novelist myself, I look to Jared Smith's poetry to start my day. I read him to remind me why writers put pen to paper: to lend insight and beauty to a world that sometimes seems scarred and broken; to recognize the singular power of words to affirm and heal; to give every individual a place in the collective whole. In his fifth decade as a poet, Jared Smith's *That's How It Is* proves as powerful and relevant as his early work—a remarkable feat in the world of poetry, one for which we should all be extremely grateful. I know I am."

—BK Loren, Author of *Theft,* winner of the Willa and the Mountains and Plains Independent Bookseller Awards

Other titles from Jared Smith:

Song Of The Blood (The Smith Press)
Dark Wing (Charred Norton Publishing)
Keeping The Outlaw Alive (Erie Street Press)
Walking The Perimeters Of The Plate Glass Window Factory
(Birch Brook Press)
Lake Michigan And Other Poems (Puddin'head Press)
Where Images Become Imbued With Time
(Puddin'head Press)
The Graves Grow Bigger Between Generations
(Higganum Hill Books)
Looking into the Machinery (Tamarack Editions)
Grassroots (Wind Publications)
The Collected Poems of Jared Smith: 1971-2011
(NYQ Books)
To the Dark Angels (NYQ Books)
This Town (Co-authored with Kyle Laws,
from Liquid Light Press)
Shadows Within The Roaring Fork (Flowstone Press)

That's How It Is

Poems by Jared Smith

Stubborn Mule Press
Devil's Elbow, MO
stubbornmulepress.com

Copyright © Jared Smith, 2019
First Edition 1 3 5 7 9 10 8 6 4 2
ISBN: 978-1-950380-47-3
LCCN: 2019944161

Design, edits and layout: Jason Ryberg
Cover and title page image: Jon Lee Grafton
Author photo: Deborah Parriott Smith
All rights reserved. No part of this publication may be reproduced or transmitted in any form or by any means, electronic or mechanical, including photocopying, recording or by info retrieval system, without prior written permission from the author.

Special thanks to the editors of the following journals, where some of these poems first appeared:

Big City Lit: "An Evening in September" and "Reflecting on Dali and the Absurd"
Casa Cinco de Hermanas: "Guitar Plucked Note by Note"
Chiron Review: "In a Street Café," "Starting With the Cadaver," "The Wild Intangibles," and "That's How it Is"
The Colorado Encyclopedia/Colorado Humanities: "That's How It Is"
Comstock Review: "As if the Wind Carried Dimensions"
Home Planet News Online: "Each Crystal Different And The Same," "Between Latitude And Longitude," "On a Stone Bench Laid Down by The CCC," "Hollow Seeds Inside The Space You Left"
Ibettson Street Review: Mr. Dick in his First Suit"
Liquid Light Press: "Inside the Glass Front Door," from the chapbook *This Town*, by Jared Smith and Kyle Laws, (Colorado, 2017)
Lummox Anthology #5. Lummox Press, "An American Worker Finding Justice"
Lyrical Somerville: "The Salt Marshes
Malpais Review: "That Night in '41," and "West 4th Above the Bait Shop"
Manifest West Anthology, (Western State University, CO, 2018,) "Like the Sun Over Primeval Earth"
Misfit Magazine: "Friends and Lovers," "Having Lived With the Muse for 50 Years," "One Note Clarion," and "The Cover of Wings"
Poetry Bay: "Rising Each Day"
Solo Novo: "With Prayers for All of Us"
Survival: A Poets Speaks Anthology (Beetlick Press Anthology, NM, 2017,) "Something Dark Beyond Words"
The Same Magazine: "The Night Marchers"
Trumped Anthology, (Beetlick Press, 2017,) "Something Dark Beyond Words"
Turtle Island Quarterly: "At the End," "In the Heart of Town" and "The Tombstones That Are Tuning Forks"

CONTENTS

Trapped Inside the Cattle Cars / 1

With Prayers for all of Us / 2

Starting With the Cadaver / 4

One Note Clarion / 5

Between Latitude and Longitude / 6

Being Part of the Birth / 7

Asking What is Missed / 8

That's How It Is / 9

An American Worker Finding Justice / 12

Where the Crops do not Grow / 14

Where This Goes on the Map / 15

Inside the Glass Front Doors / 16

I Walk Into a Whaling Hotel on West 4th / 18

The Night Marchers / 20

Rising Each Day / 22

West 4th Above the Bait Shop / 24

Arriving There / 26

Somewhere in the Mountains of America / 27

Walking Free / 30

The Salt Marshes / 31

That Night in '41 / 33

One of our Residents / 35

The Wild Intangibles / 36

The Fault is Mine as a Poet and a Man / 37

Something Dark Beyond Words / 39

As it all Drops Away / 40

Reflecting on Dali and the Absurd / 41

Underneath the University / 42

The Storm Upon Us / 43

How the Mythology and Lies Began / 44

And Life Going on Unknown / 47

On a Stone Bench Laid Down by the CCC / 49

Most Things / 51

As Reported by The BBC in December of 2017 / 52

As if the Wind Carried Dimensions / 53

Meadows Where You Walk / 54

Just a Fistful of Change / 56

Mr. Dick in his First Suit / 58

Dear Microbes With Your March / 59

The Cover of Wings / 60

In the Community of Trust / 61

Taking What the West Winds Spawn / 62

It is a Strong Wind / 64

Is This to Sing / 65

Like the Sun Over Primeval Earth / 66

In a Street Café / 68

The Tombstones That are Tuning Forks / 69

When the Storm Came Upon Us / 70

The Light is Different / 71

Each Crystal Different and the Same / 72

What a Sunset It Is! / 73

An Evening in September / 74

Friends and Lovers / 75

Guitar Plucked Note by Note / 76

A Gathering of Ghosts / 77

In Wilderness There is no Virtue / 79

Having Lived With the Muse for 50 Years / 81

Outside Caribou / 82

Tributaries / 83

Fishing Below Timberline / 84

Here in the West / 85

That Time of Year the West is Best Defined / 86

Hollow Seeds Inside the Space You Left / 88

At the End / 90

So Like the Metal Cattle Cars / 91

Beneath The Heavy, Slow Machinery / 92

This is the American Dream, and What of Joe / 93

That's How it Is

For verses are not, as people imagine, simply feelings (those one has early enough), —they are experiences. For the sake of a single verse, one must see many cities, men and things, one most know the animals, one must feel how the birds fly and know the gesture with which the little flowers open in the morning. One must be able to think back to roads in unknown regions, to unexpected meetings and to partings one had long seen coming; to days of childhood that are still unexplained, to parents whom one had to hurt when they brought one some joy and one did not grasp it (it was a joy for someone else); to childhood illnesses that so strangely begin with such a number of profound and grave transformations, to days in rooms withdrawn and quiet and to mornings by the sea, to the sea itself, to seas, to nights of travel that rushed along on high and flew with all the stars—and it is not yet enough if one may think of all this. One must have memories of many nights of love, none of which was like the others, of the screams of women in labor, of light, white, sleeping women in childbed, closing again. But one must also have been beside the dying, must have sat beside the dead in the room with the open window and the fitful noises. And still it is not yet enough to have memories. One must be able to forget them when they are many and one must have the great patience to wait until they come again. For it is not yet the memories themselves. Not till they have turned to blood within us, to glance and gesture, nameless and no longer to be distinguished from ourselves—not till then can it happen that in a most rare hour the first word of a verse arises in their midst and goes forth from them.

—Rilke

Trapped Inside the Cattle Cars

Trapped inside the cattle cars
one is aware of the gentle warmth of flesh
and the leaning into each other,
the comfort of the rocking cradle.
We have each other for support.
The iron rails seem to last forever.

With Prayers for All of Us

Some men are not formed to stoke the machines
that build the cement and steel cells we live in,
and some are born in the vales without factories,
are born with voices sent from the wings of angels,
are not able to turn their dreams to data points,
are soft and gentle in this mighty flow sweeping us
away into the wilderness we know without boundaries.

The poppies of Flanders Field have now come to this,
their pure, sad juices cut by industrial poisons,
the eyes of goddesses misplaced in sterile rooms
pushing back against the pain of too much poverty,
pushing back against the division of class, of majesty,
refurnishing dreams that will not last a lifetime,
pushing back against all where the war is always lost.

The door is open and people make their choices,
and some soldiers go out now instead of in sweatshops.
Some give in to the siren call. Some stop their ears,
tied to their ship like Ulysses' Argonauts, gold-fleeced
and bound to the structures they have built for another.

And each man, each woman, each thought and dream
is sacred with the scent of sun breathed into flesh
caught and swirled upon this mighty sea of life,

so why and how can we assume to be the gods
that tie their hands to the mast when we are far from home
and we are hurrying there driven by the winds that bind?

Starting With the Cadaver

      and peeling it apart
                knots in the veins are not
wired bunches but are valves the first-year anatomist learns
opening and closing the flow of fluid understanding
      the love of soft scented flesh
      the chorus of spring afternoons
      the brittle bitter bits of machinery
supporting lungs and bowels and dreams.

We know this because we study the dead.
They are the software of our cities, the plans that were flesh,
turned over and melted down into templates, their openings
and closings, their capturing of the fluidity of spaces,
their body electrics singing the song beyond themselves
      and peeling it apart
                the veins become hydraulic valves
in elevated cranes lifting rooftops and bridge overhangs
      replaceable when the metal rusts out
            we have learned so much.

One Note Clarion

A life of dawns had gone by
and papers yellowed by file cabinets
data driven onto disks and forgotten
mountains climbed and floods survived
before Lazarus felt he'd pretty much seen
and felt and known what there was to see,
and he lay at the darkest time of night.
Nothing to say. Nothing new to know,
when the first bird of day at 3 a.m. spoke
one note that echoed off the stones surrounding
giving shape to each shattered shard of earth.
A simple note of chaos from feathered memory
piercing understanding, a note remembered
from the nest, a word learned from inside the egg
which once learned brought first light then food
from all in nature that could be woven for warmth.
A life of dawns gone by and yet it pierces
and is a note he realizes slowly that lights the sun,
that shapes the branches, that give wing to life,
and so he rises again knowing he knows nothing
and begins to bring these new notes and thoughts
together in a book of psalms and songs and poems
unholy and important as anything a life might give.

Between Latitude and Longitude

Driving a city highway you are the long thin neural network
running the spinal column of the body electric,
each streetlamp a vertebrae
                each office light a node
each apartment in each high rise condominium
       an input expanding around itself
that you gather into your awareness.
At its core, love is a gazillion bar stools
in ten quadrillion states of mind in the cloud
       forward
backward across time held static
               hyperlinked perplexity real time.

A car moves toward a tiny town of 200 souls
in western Colorado at 10 p.m.
and the driver is a compound of mountains
with a handful of kitchens, wood burning stoves for heat
he is aware of the Earth and not the grid,
of the network of rivers into lakes and time.

A plane passes over the country
each light below it human consciousness
dreams in a very distant night that breathes.
You think that you are flying the plane
       just as every other passenger
in all this vastness you follow the lines
and you are on the grid.

Being Part of the Birth

The egg is so bright where it shatters
       its inconsequential shell all but invisible
            ova extends transcends paths of being
   into beyond being but it just stays there
smearing the concrete plane it descended to
    from its nest
but each string of yoke immediately feeds a multitude
           lighting them up for seconds
bestowing existence where a moment ago there was none

and so from nothing
      in the moment the fetus dies
           a question rises in those mouths that think
   before being extinguished in what stays there
about where the golden food that came comes from
and where the strands of dying light lead to
    from its nest
something vastly larger feathery and perhaps foul
           perhaps angelic
must have come before that great bang and expansion
       into who or what remembers in all the arcs of
comprehension.

Asking What is Missed

What is it determines which molecule of water within the river rises next into mist, or is carried away invisibly into the air between these strings of willow? What determines the path of which molecule of life is drained from the depths of this river into the roots of those trees along its bank, lingers there briefly, and then too goes off into the air between those branches that wave toward a distant sun they cannot see. Which molecules among all the rest while breaking down mountains carry the earth all the way to a distant sea, and what do they carry of the rest of those that now are lost, and of those which are lost what remains of them as they reform and soak down upon another continent…what hydrogen, what oxygen, what glue that bound them and might have filled our lips. They are as bound together and loose as the sands upon our shores and all the elements of all the rocks on which we stand and multiplied by all the stars beyond our sky. What salt or temperate current swept them to which end and which beginning.

That's How It Is

Sunrise finds the New York shopkeepers rolling up their windows
dusting off the counters sweeping the floors shoveling their walkways
pulling pastries from dry hot ovens filling coffee pots to get the morning going
for the secretaries and executives and lawyers bankers insurance salesmen clerks
and the homeless too coming in quietly with their handfuls of fear and empty bellies
because it's another day, and the workers do what workers do every blessed day
not too aware of what they do or whom they serve but it's morning and they rise

and sunrise is indifferent as the clouds and passes on to Pennsylvania
and it reflects redness off the empty steel mills and foundries
where again the shopkeepers rise and here the miners line up for unemployment
or the lucky ones still do down into the darkness of the earth with fear in their hearts
and fishermen line up on the banks of the Alleghany with their thermoses
and a gum chewing girl from a diner clears egg-smeared plates from tables
watching the traffic that never ends go by along the interstate a seamless zipper

and sunrise hurries on its way out across the freighters on Lake
    Michigan
and the commodity traders working screaming toward heart
    attacks in Chicago
the endowed institutions of learning that line our cities the
    students half asleep
out over the heartland where the grain still grows so high it never
    touches the ground
and on out over eastern and then western Kansas where the
    aquifers are drying
and the promise of America's breadbasket is starting to grow thin

it moves on across the mountains of Colorado, hiding itself in
    valleys
and pointing out the oil wells and ore dumps and abandoned
    ghost towns
the rusting scaffolding of the Roan Plateau the toxic sumps of
    Climax
and the shopkeepers rising to open their shops for the clerks and
    lawyers
ranchers driving their herds to the high country or to the low
    country
                        depending on the season
it changes but sunrise moves across it and as always work begins
and sunrise has no mind no consciousness of the shadows growing
and of how the same work has to start and be filled each day or
of the darkness that follows only hours behind and the light
behind that the tired muscles in a man's arms the panic

at the morning table when the bills come out
the liquor sparkling in taverns after the day in gone
shimmering in the folds of evening gowns but
it moves on without reference to the thoughts of workers

sunrise brightens up the sands of Vegas and the roulette
    tables
the hookers high-rollers and papers in the gutters along
    the strip
the hangovers and empty wallets left over from the night
    before
and the shop owners the police the judges putting on
    their pants
the hotel windows glinting back a desert sandscape to the sky
but it moves on and peeks upon the Hollywood sign and the
cougar living in those hills and the movie makers making
    reality
and flattens out over the iron endless gray of the Pacific
but even as the surf is up off California it is growing darker
to the east and the day is as long as the motions we all go
    through.

An American Worker Finding Justice

The stress of leaving home each year as time
went on across each stretch of concrete
pushing a pen or pressing computer keys
across ten hours of office floors a day and
selling vacation homes to the god-given,
taking the hits of being a bastard in a suit
or of hammering the god-given Earth
for flesh breaking hours of jackhammers
because I've done whatever it is one does
with BMers throwing up mud in my face
and the cold wave of horror of no job at all
takes a toll that's grown slow in my blood,
I know. It's what you do. It's what we do.
I've checked the Kaiser website
and I know the number of years I've lost
to the playboy one percent, but it's for a
girl I used to carry on my knee at five
and for a son I took on evening hikes
and for the colleges they were sent to
and my wife and what it did to her as well,
it's that bitterness and rage I carry now
hardening inside my arteries, that plaque that
is placed on the chest of every American worker,
marking each of us as the last hero to stand
where the road finally runs out into silhouette

and the shadow of words that beckon us home.
And tonight as I stand here before the sunset
and its rays suffuse me and I stand beneath stars
I am filled with a peace I do not understand,
and call this justice, for it is what we share.

Where the Crops do not Grow

Crops are not growing where they grew last year
        where the dust grows
there are no fish swimming in the mountain streams
no longer fed by glaciers that hang above our valley
   streams where the dust flows
and it is growing colder than anyone can imagine
        where the sun burns our skin
writing histories in shadows and charcoal
the seasons change beyond the pages of our books.

Any season at all will hold if it does not disrupt itself
        thermophilic bacteria Sulphur eaters icemen cometh
where they have time to plant their sporadic seeds
if they do the twisted and unwanted the hind one unadapted
   will survive and become as you are now—
hunter and gatherer sublime where the crops do not grow.

Where This Goes on the Map

I don't know where this goes on the map,
what little lines or abstract symbols give it its worth.
I don't know how asteroids impacting on planets
change its meaning, though I suspect not much.
I don't know how the flow of money and politics
will affect your flesh or progeny, but I do know this:
These are the lines that are not set by the fates,
but are the ones that you find scuffing your feet
barefoot in the alleys behind the houses where you grew
where the streetlamps were shattered by the homeless
and the broken glass shattered their shadows at dawn.

I know that these are the maps that matter now
when you have gone so far from what your learned.

Inside the Glass Front Doors

The golden retriever is almost a fixture
beneath a corner table in the back of the cafe,
sprawled out and with tongue lolling, taking
everything in lying on the floor half asleep,
but with head raised between an old man's legs.
He catalogues the day the way that dogs do,
the people coming in through open doors and closed,
the way the eggs come in each morning from the back
with the rancid, titillating smell of chickens
and how those that eat them come in the front.
How the bacon comes in with another man formed
around the full-bodied smell of pigs and grains.
The chicken man has grains too. Perhaps grain is
somehow drawn to the back doorway, the worn
wood doorway with paint chipped off. He faces
toward the food-way. But he takes in the rest,
and hears the car too fast down Main Street,
the rattling of machinery, whoop of sirens,
smells the sea that surrounds us all and dozes
knowing lying between his man's legs all is well,
and that the woman who brings food will come
and each plate will carry easy over eggs and toast
and that cups of coffee will slowly light each table
and a bottomless pan of water will appear as it does.
He has no names for these things but knows them
as every creature, every part of Town, knows itself.

A fly comes in off one of the old fishing boats
harbored days away and says meaningless about his ears.
Dog raises a paw and kicks his head, and the fly goes on
about his business one plate of food at a time, its eyes
seeing the way that the eyes of flies see in multitudes
so that each person coming in to eat at Mom's Cafe
brings maybe a thousand more with him, all the same
bringing food in the backdoor and taking it out the front
and smiling with teeth that could take your wings off
while handing life to each other on old chipped plates.
It's Sunday morning, but that doesn't mean much:
The whole town comes by in multitudes each day
as sun begins to bake the pavements hot outside,
and the coffee grinder mimics the sound of all machines
in so many dimensions that a fly cannot keep track.
It's okay because life goes on with wings on a full belly
and one doesn't suppose anyone sees anything really
but ghosts and shadows and metal cash registers
and the dry soil still speaking of Dust Bowl memories
  and little Towns and Urban Centers
and something that is bigger than dogs or old men
or even memories that keep right on filling their days.

I Walk Into a Whaling Hotel on West 4th

Whatever you perceive becomes real.
Whatever you have words for becomes what
  you understand.

I walk into an old whaling hotel on West 4th Street
and climb a spiral staircase to the third floor
where I open a door that has pinhole cameras in it,
cross a studio apartment and sit at a typewriter
with the kind of keys you have to bang hard on
and a little carriage that rattles in the wind of time
as I pour trees of cheap paper through its gears.

There are those who try to get in. I can hear them
in the hard banging of the radiator, the scratches
at the door where the landlord threatens to break in,
the tapping on the window when a young woman
who descended the fire escape enters on a cold night
and presses her fingers to her lips, says don't say
anything and takes her clothes off then mine
but the carriage keeps on keeping on and in days
I am one more memory kept outside of her Detroit
and there are no words ever written of or by her.

And the windows are always open so some nights
a battered woman with her two nighthawks is there
and at times an old professor boils soup bones

to a clear broth in pewter bowls with China spoons
and despite the storms and snow blowing outside
and drifting in across my books and pillows it is hot.
This is the way it is and she was shot at Kent State
and my body blew across empty cities for years
and the mountains were too far away in all that time,
the commuter trains of briefcases too close and fast.

A place so holy that there were monsters at each stop
where the subways ended and the stars burned through
and I walked alone among all the silken shrouds
where men who were men once hung their oak harpoons
as the city laid stone to be their cold brick homes,
and yet it was warm and magical inside…soft music
and the scent of life starting out now anew on time

Cash-in the cache of clay pigeons.
Clouds betoken change,
the swelling of cities, the passing of generations,
the illumining of those things that are unseen,
and they came again that evening
or was it that the sun grew covered
that mushrooms sprouted in the ivy-covered hall
but whatever, the winds were far above us
circling on the wings of vultures for a fortnight,
and we thought we recognized our voices,
that we still could scent each other's bodies,

and so it was.

The Night Marchers

There are certain streets you don't walk down,
streets where half the lights are blown out and
shadows warm their hands around old oil cans,
places where the street is just too narrow, too
closely guarded by dry graffitied sliding doors
so seldom seen the signs might mean anything.

These are the streets college students ignore
going to and from late night classroom lectures,
the streets that even taxi drivers stay away from
and homeless people tell of the darkness that waits
and of the muted crying they hear at midnight.
They are where bones are discovered at dawn.

Not that you have ever been there. You have
passed with a nervous glance back into the shadows,
perhaps have tightened your fist around your keys
so that one key protrudes like a switchblade knife
between the cold fingers clenched within your pocket
and you hurry back toward the artificial lights.

Sometimes lying awake before the night recedes
you can hear the dreadful roar of universes clashing
perhaps coming from these corners of the city and
you say as you wake it is the garbage trucks coming,
clanging and banging, barging their way through,
sweeping away the mountains of debris we build,
and sometimes it is, but that's only what you think.

It is the same in each city, as the police records indicate,
there are the unsolved mysteries and murders the lost
mostly sequestered together down these darkened lanes
near where the heavy tankers come in by warehouses.
And it's true too in the small forgotten mid west towns
where along one dusty lane a farmer's home has gone to dust
his family disappeared within the holes that line the house,
that house that even small children stay away from now,
the cage now keeping something in and something out
while people sleep and beings from other dimensions enter
perhaps as dreams and perhaps as something else entirely.

Rising Each Day

After you've been at it for awhile
your hands stop bleeding, calluses
harden and shoulders become pistons
powering through the pain to become
your image of the iconic steel driver
rolling perpetual motion beneath mountains
rolling in the summer sunset clouds burned
with the soul of Christ's blood and tears,
and what you hear in the bark of words
and the grunts of flesh alongside your own
is your muscle matched against the stones
you break down for houses, metals, jewels
that are sold alongside the Palace of the Governors
after you've been at it for awhile,
after the song is in your blood, your love in your arms,
and your flesh picks up the scent of dreams
stored in the acrid gears of accountability,
and the clean bit air fills your lungs
each morning into infinity after awhile.

Mi casa not much more than a stucco barn
or a packing case for heavy iron machinery,
but calm within itself and me within itself,
turning over peaceful one last time in my bed
and hearing a train whistle set to wake the dead
scattering the coyotes among the sage brush,

echoing the testes of neighborhood roosters
fanning their feathers in arroyo dust, these
were the dreams with hard bright eyes and
long necks hung out for the chopping block,
but oh, that mountain air was so sweet, and
enough to make pinon coffee break the sleep,
and I would pack my lunch pail each day
with all that I could fit into its dark light sides
and step out into a burning sun that blinded me
with the repetition and singing not so bad each
day where the starting whistle echoed the trains
that filled each night, that carried the stone I broke,
with my shoulders the wheels of industry and love
rolling across this endless horizon that connects us all.

West 4th Above the Bait Shop

Richard lives on West 4th Street above the bait shop.
He hates the flies that keep him awake all summer, hates
the way they see the world, hates their endless hunger but
he paints the town in excruciating detail in oils on wood,
brush strokes and palette knife gouging out and scraping
away the shadows, painting wide-eyed angels on street corners,
their faces worn and the shade of storm sails, eyes blood red
reaching out toward the viewer as he sees them every day,
their wings folded around their shoulders like woolen scarves,
their features the knotholes of old willows gone away.

We've had our share of talks because he knows something
about the history of mankind whether he's right or wrong
and I can hear the music beating in my head as he talks, and
the colors he uses, the pigments he pulls from the earth
are not like the ones they sell in artists' stores or schools.
I call him Dick, but quietly not to give offense because
he's a painter who paints with the land and has a harpoon
hanging on the wall behind his bed and talks with demons
no one else can see but we can't see the angels either and
their eyes reach out to us with all the pain we had forgotten
that separated us from each other and the stars at night.

Downstairs a heavy new flat of sandworms has been delivered. Shiners are sweeping end to end in an arc across a metal tank, their sides shimmering with the darkness of early morning, catching the first rays of light gathering outside the windows moving as one soul the door opens and a bell rings the door closes and the voices of people begin to fill the air.

Arriving There

There are no straight lines in nature
nor are there in thought.
The buildings you live in, yes.
The mountains around them, no.
The math connecting corridors, yes.
The math connecting galaxies, no.
Your thought launched in a Great Circle
on your words is the most direct path
whether it takes a lifetime of emotion
or a day in infinity is all the same in time.

Somewhere in the Mountains of America

Where sun hits water the mind
    kaleidoscopes
  wind pressing liquid to my thighs
overtures of leaves
  budded and grown and torn swept by wind
swirling the surface
     rolled along gravel
  collected
in this stream I stand encased in neoprene waders
in sight of where the ice fields melt into August
where caddis flies collect spring's debris
     carry it on their backs as camouflage
caught in the current pressed to my groin
pulsating the times of our lives in fractals
       now digitals
dancing the waves of a brisk, cold wind;
Shiners catching the sun as it dips,
     swirling in schools as one
above the dark trout I seek to stab with feathers
somewhere between the tightening of line and water
  where the computer cannot catch the flesh,
I am mired though walking through the waters
    sound of cars still on the highway
the mountain willows dropping memory
  the cormorants diving and emerging
       a distant scent of barbecue

oil of machinery driving the factories
across the pure white flesh of young women--
all washing down in the glacier's memories.

The steel in my lip
  the lead dragging down of my lungs
    the oxygen that gives me life
      the eyes that fill my belly
the scales that armor my sides and
waters that I read through shifts in current
tumbling along the outcrops that build America
mention 120 killed Parisians, 300 Pakistanis, 600 Syrians,
on this day the trout ate on what was there

and I caught nothing while the sun set
and lightening came closer along the peaks
that lie above the waters I call home.

I call home the subways of New York
and the graffiti covered abandoned stations
no one knows what lies beneath the city
I call home the Petri dishes of laboratories
where men and women wear white coats
and for the price of a parking ticket men work,
raising their families and bloodlust on oatmeal
grown in oats beneath the sun before factorized
and splendorized beneath media's eyes despair.

I am merely a fisherman
here in America
tying my tackle as I have been taught
where the rivers run out of the mountains
out of steel and gold and molybdenum and feathers,
and the clouds are silvered with evening's rust,
and I want to feel the struggle against flesh,
but I'm thinking of my woman too, and of my son,
and I'm wanting to take home something
they can sink their teeth into, something of the sun
settling beyond the mountains I see only in silhouette,
yet which will test the strength of my arms, America,
and will fit into the creel I carry on my belt
America and I sigh looking up into the stars above.

Walking Free

This is the time shadows gather.
I walk outside my neighbor's fences
wide awake with the scent of earth.
The sky is distant and red with time,
the streetlamps reminders of a time
when crime was committed in person.
With no place to go I approach home,
a state of mind beyond the media
that encroaches.   There are crickets
in the dark that sense my passage
and their song will last beyond me.
There is a music one can hear
when all the cars and trading slows.
Not everything within me is made of light.
Not everything casts shadows.

The Salt Marshes

Beyond the doctor's offices, real estate brokers. greasy diners,
beyond the houses, there were the salt marshes themselves
shifting back and forth, waving on all sides outside the town filled
with the smell of stranded fish and overabundance of clams,
broken shells, sandworms, bloodworms, fiddler crabs,
and the steel grey of herons wading waiting in the evening
knowing that from this flatness one could pluck flashes of silver
and carry them off into the sunset as if they had never been.

I got to know those marshes, as I knew the heavy smell of horses
that came to permeate my clothes, though they were not water horses
and had to be left tied to the bones of cypress knees at the end
   of the beach
when I wanted to wander halfway inland and roll up my pant
   legs, feel
the earth oozing up between my toes as I walked to the inner
   island,
more a raised sand bar than an island, but with vegetation, a tree
where ospreys landed in the daytime and a great horned owl at night,
where the bones of fish and rodents lay scattered in a bleached heap,
perhaps the leftovers of meals or the beginnings of land or both.

When the wind howled from the ocean or Town itself grew too close,
when the wizened stub fingered fishermen drank too much at the bar
and began bragging of all the things they had dredged from their nets

as the moon rose in the evening those marshes would be my shelter, and I would walk out into them beneath the blank eyes of the owl, and I would know that the grasses had eyes and the soil itself a soul. This was separate from where I lived, of course, but it was there contained within the ribcage of a vessel that knew the night unafraid.

That Night in '41

It was their eyes that always got me,
flat and unblinking as dinner plates
or as the coins we traded in markets,
but come from the deep with something
horrible endless dredged up to the light,
to be thrown dead naked on dinner plates.
You eat what you can get, I know, but
the scales themselves catch in your throat
when everything you eat comes from dark
and is drawn to the light you spread, and
nothing comes from the land you can see.

That night the blossoms bloomed at sea was
like so many nights our lads set the nets
and lit the diesel driven lights above them,
and the ever hungry water hissed beneath,
as the nets played out and the shrimp rose
drawn to an artificial dawn, and the great fish,
those that knew the eternal darkness of life,
rose to the light that filled their lidless eyes
and thrashed in the final spectacle of death
drawn to the elusive light that gave them life,
trapped thrashing into a world of demons,

The blossoms bloomed at sea distant while
I watched, first one and then an hour later another,
so that I held my girl in wonder on the beach
asking what was that and what was that, holding
each other's hands as we watched the fairy lights
those trawlers carried on their rigging burst,
becoming flames that lit those floating cities
on the beaches back in October of 1941. The next
day, that fast, the trawlers knew to dark their lights
but the bodies of some of our Town-folk came in
smelling of the world of commerce and of Europe
and their eyes like those of fish filled with memory.

We read then of the U-Boats off the coast of Coney Island
at night and the shape of freighters caught in the light
of amusement parks, and we learned to eat less
like the Great Depression that blew in from Arizona
and filled the sky over Washington. We were afraid,
but still town is town and you do what you must do.

One of our Residents

One of our residents went missing.
There is a dark pool in her backyard.
Security cameras last showed her running
naked in the courtyard of the arms cafe.
Nothing clumsy or heavy bottomed, but
supple as a dancer's shadow on a grave.
All the tapes have been confiscated twice,
and there is a shining halo at the far left.
No witnesses were left to say her skin
was pure as the white stone marble
outside the edifice she called home.

The Wild Intangibles

There is no art taught in the universities.
    There is no poetry, now no song
        but the wind rubbing grains of sand
and the sand's percussion against rock
and the tear of bits of stone against flesh.
    These are the music
unfettered and untold.
There are the mountains, their slow heaving
as they churn storm clouds above the valley.
The squirrels scratching outside my window
where shades are pulled back and sun dances
along the frozen spines of forgotten books.
Their pages turn and my sorrow reaches out.
There is no art taught in the universities.
    There is no poetry, no song,
        there are no children
among the workers laying roads and factories
building bridges from one capitol dome to another
there are no times for hyacinths blooming
    the wolf calling his mate
        the wild intangibles.

The Fault is Mine as a Poet and a Man

When does a man leave-off responsibility
for his life's shape and his family, despite having
struggled his professional life fighting terrorism
in the name of his government, his upbringing, beliefs,
at the end of his disposal period in the name of media,
when the cheap, cliché definitions of that mass media
which he fought against because they had no meaning
for decades in his life when he was scared to walk alone
suddenly come down to wealthy aristocrats turning terrorist
and butchering people in downtown America, *mal pais*
   badlands,
I am talking about your state of death in the year of our Lord
and I am talking of my state of death in the past decades,
when does a man leave off responsibility when the mad
mass media has taken over the language of bureaucracy
with the acronyms of weapons of mass destruction and
jihad nihilism and government has stopped its ears
when does a man leave off responsibility for tuning out
and protecting his family with the wealth of words.
When does a poet who is more than an entertainer stop
wearing the shawls of poverty and perversion and
take his stand to say people are people. This is what I know
and have spent all the years of my life walking the streets
and chewing the stale bread of diplomacy for knowing and
trying to speak of to the lords of science and power and
   technology,

this is what the dogs lying in the gutters would tell you of,
and what I have given up trying to tell you of, but I must,
even though you shunt me off into forgotten cafes with ghosts,
I must come back now to haunt you with the truth of words
you have never known in your technological hearts,
    Americans,
when I lie awake each night not knowing where to turn or how
to step off-stage at the poetry festivals and say I am a man
in words that build not machinery or wealth but the space
    between stars.

Something Dark Beyond Words

There is something waiting in the autumn woods
there ahead right there beyond that crest that hollow
where shadows blend its red claws into the leaves.
You can smell it…something musky on the air
and it beats its massive paws up and down, a trumpeting
and tramping wholly out of place along this casual path,
but it waits for no one and it waits for anyone and
its roaring shakes the earth beneath your feet
and its drumming haunts the dreams of better men
and its drumming wakes its neighbors who start to sing
and they sing of blood and feathers and they sing
of armies trudging forward and they sing of earth
claiming what the seasons bring it out of time
and it's right there up ahead where the crest is
and you can smell it in the air and taste it on your tongue
and revulsion comes to claim you, pulls you back
from that path along the river where the leaves are turning
colors and you shrink into the shadows but it drags you
from your soul and it pulls out all your words and drips
them in the river scattered by the seasons and you
wish for better men and women but they cry
and run when they see you on that path by the river
there is something in the woods and it is coming it is
no longer waiting in the pages of past history it is
darkness for the country and will burn out our tomorrows
and we have no trumpet to blow down its walls and fences
that were whispers in the wind not so very long ago.

As It All Drops Away

Aphrodite
in all the nakedness
she was painted in
holds a clamshell
to her ear and hears
the great nothing

Reflecting on Dali and the Surreal

Even in Dali's four dimensional sculpture
of enlarged Jesus hanging on a cross over Mary
there is not a hair on his chest or belly nothing
but that which covers the face, nor is there any
painting or depiction I can recall that does, and
as a man who felt the world through his moustache
like a catfish feeling for dimension off the bottom
and who had hair all over himself I wonder as I, like
Dali, think of all of time which drips off everything
glance down along my arm to my hairy wristwatch
why there was so little hair on the rest of him and
as I get somewhat older there gets to be less on me
and what might have happened if Jesus got a bit older
or if I had not made it to the age of sixteen or so myself
which was when I began to let my beard grow out.

It is four in the morning
and the smallest bird can wake the world.

Underneath the University

Geologic time runs neither slow nor fast,
but with the seasons of flood, earth tremor, magma
shifting the slow drift of pollen among evergreens.

The Storm Upon Us

The winds blow differently
through the hot dry cities this year
and the tombstones that were apartment houses
are wind chimes that no one listens to. The streets
which were going nowhere before now are empty,
children thrown forward through their own windshields.

And the winds blow differently out across the ocean,
weighing more as they drop the human ash they carry
in torrid, whipping hurricanes that breathe out death,
and the hollow skulls of wise men chatter in their rooms
as the winds flicker in and out through lidless eyes.

And the winds blow differently in the mountains too,
carving canyons among the new formed craters
and among the burned grasses of the high plains
and along the eaves of little houses hidden off the grid
where the poorest of us all still hold out and wait
afraid and with their arms about each other wait
for the hard hot rain that will come to them even to them
      before the winds too die out and
no man or animal remarks upon the time at all.

How the Mythology and Lies Began

I want to find out with you
how the mythology we are living in took root
and with you destroy the monsters who control us,
and I hope that you will take this to your heart
and talk of it over the dinner table
and take it to the office and refuse
as I have done, I swear, to work for the computers
and stop entertaining yourself on the conglomerate
that alienates your children and family from you
and remember what it is like to drink to the stars
and to walk with your lover beneath the stars
and know that you are part of a family of friends
and that all of you are born of the stars and
the data controlling man today is nothing
but magnetic impulses that melt to time.

I want to find out with you
what Eisenhower meant in his dotage
when he was at his majesty in his retiring
from the world stage when he warned of
the military industrial complex, how
he who had led that miscarriage of sanity
from a small Midwest American town, he
who had led the massacre of American farmers
along with General MacArthur before the War
and yet we see now well into the loss of The

American Dream, who burned out a tent town
of protesting farmers whose families were starving
before he defeated the totalitarians of World War
and led the armies of democracy across all Europe,
what the hell did he know that burned those farmers
who left their farms and families to drive to Washington,
that scared him so much that he abandoned the Midwest
even as he tried to keep Democracy alive in America?

I want to find out with you who owns this thing we call
The Land of the Free and how they came in possession of it,
How they deceived those people who drove the plow or
cheated/corrupted/scammed those who wrote our symphony,
I want to find out and share this with you and do what you will
remembering that men and women are not all the same or
   irreplaceable
and that something changed the General that saved us all,
and that scared him enough that he turned on us before
he saved us in the War that would save mankind,
and I want to share my experience of life with you
and my loves and lovers and my hates and terror,
and I want to ask you what changed the mythology
we live with today and what can we do to remain alive.

The mythology we live in now has metal gods
with brittle edges, not the gods of passion, Ares or Venus,
war or love, but rather of containment, of measured control,
of data compiled by those that drove the Axis in WWII
and by those that thought somehow they had the answers,
that magnetic impulses on plastic were greater than the soul.
I want to know and to talk with you and to turn this back.

When I worked with our National Laboratories during the 1990s
as a Special Advisor of The Administration and the Pentagon, I
was asked to tell our national leaders where our resources lay—
our gold, our natural gas and oil, our electric power grids—
and to find the perfect data grids I had to go to German data
and to companies owned by the great steel companies and
    financiers
who powered Germany under Hitler in WWII, who had the data
and knew that the data still ruled if only one believed it did,
and I saw that their family names and corporate ownership
were the same now as they were then and I was afraid and quit,
and I have been changed by that as have others who could not
    talk, and
in anger went into the mountains and watched the continental shift,
and thought if there are gods they too shift and one becomes
    another or not
and said that if there are any answers they are in the age of the earth
and if I am to understand them I must observe them deeply
and must talk at length with others who do also
and I want to understand so that this false mythology does not last.

And Life Going on Unknown

Such sudden stillness
at the end of a season of fire and flood
at the end of a life too short
     always too short
for each lost yearning
of life walked beneath the stars
the cold ice of November melted
on the alpine peaks washed down
through ash accumulated years
in torrents geologic time sometimes
beyond nightmare moves fast,
and last night too was lost
as the mountain came down
upon her house, and I think
there may have been an instant
of awareness that all was ending.

The roads gone now,
the loved rocks and masonry
a wall piled above her eyes
in the valley she resides in night
as a mound of lost memory
we probe with metal rods
in waste deep mud torn hands
clothes lost to geologic history,
and I can't think of how to call

our mother who lies also back east
in a hospital room her eyes closed
with metal tubes going in what
good could come of telling her
of her family even if we could

now after the pings of the EKG
and the mindless roar of the MRI
trying to discern the shape of tumors
that grow beneath the flesh of Mrs. or Mr.
separate from what made hope or dreams
separate from what gave life to love
from what made this awful absence
so much a part of what lies here
where the universe comes together
with meaning at the end of night,
the roads gone now and life going on
probing among the ashes that remain.

On a Stone Bench Laid Down by the CCC

Western Pennsylvania man, Erie County,
sitting on a stone bench he carved in
the mythology of America, he knew it
took the broken bedrock of men's lives
to break and shape the bedrock of Colorado,
the song of failed wheat fields and factories,
the failure of Capitalism and Communism,
the triumph of a bully, a dozen madmen,
a bureaucracy built from the failure of all
at the eastern ends of where the railways ran
carrying the hobos and failures westward,
the men who traded nothing to test their arms
to beat against the earth itself in rage and hope
collapsing as a band of brothers and singers
and shapers of a future built of stone…No,
built of a world where flowers and cabins,
walkways and drives built along the edge of sky
where nothing could be seen except the world
itself rolling with the ageless continents was
measurable even though they worked alone
it was enough to send a few nickels home
and enough to keep their wives and children
living long enough to forget what their fathers
eventually would give their lives for…now
turning their eyes toward metal finance and
data driven media our past did not dream nor need…

from Pennsylvania Ohio Oklahoma from Europe
and Asia and everywhere the adventurous failed,
from where the heart of America still had room to beat,
these men caught in the sweep of song and hope set
out across our country, building dreams of stone huts
and of parkways built through mountain passes
all across America, but never more than here in
Colorado where mountains separated man from soul
until they could be sculpted tunneled drilled driven
across the bedrock and the alpine fields opened out…

a nation back then, our nation back then funded that
and out of that the oil and gold that drives us today,
but what of the brotherhood of men that drove them…
too many gone too many bought too few alive today.

Most Things

Most things done by man can be undone by time,
                and no one knows
the heavy grunt of machinery moving these hills
the cars sweat urgent phone calls weapons tests
the dry lines worn into hopeless homeless faces
the jackpot at the end of the rainbow not here but
before these mountains beneath these glaciers
where the trill of alpine rills rings rock to rock
and a setting sun this evening lights the world
with the last thoughts of coins and evening gowns
some things matter more than others, and we
keep on in our little ways, and maybe thirty years
from now or a million the spores from this fern
nestled against my hiking boots may grow green
in a place not dreamed of now, but where they will
                and no one knows.

As Reported by the BBC

200,000 species of dust mite and fungi
slough off each human body into homes each day,
dropping away to hide under beds,
billowing away beneath bookcases,
slipping into the fabric of rugs and clothes,
70,000,000 mites and yeasts per hour per body,
your skin a veritable jungle of eat and be eaten,
and yet you say you don't make a difference.

As if the Wind Carried Dimensions

The sand slips beneath my feet half
step back for each step forward small
stones rolling under my shoes I can
hear the creak of harness in the wind
solid spoked wheels turning heaving
horses' ragged breathing into desert
wind whipping the canvas walls as
wagon after wagon crosses time and
Fred barks orders from up ahead
turning the train toward water as I
bend and grab one hand of sand into
the air, just one hand of sand, one
and suddenly a wind that knows no
source blasts a tornado of earth smoke,
like something I might have dreamed
that stings my eyes like last night's
fire and fills the nostrils, such a small
token taken from the land by my hand,
and I shudder, bend into the wind as
if something heavy and faster than air
or the passage of time was upon us
coming down from the distant hills,
and Sarah's voice calls to me John
what is this thing that comes sudden,
as if the landscape were alive with time?

Meadows Where You Walk

Once were there meadows where you walk
once were there little lives and little deaths
once otters played by the creek that flowed
across the street from this midnight diner
where we share our wine and once again
our time is a time to know that even concrete
fails to cover the streams that flow beneath
and that where meadows bloomed they will
once again in the passage of time once we
have danced our dance and sung our song
where deer sipped from the waters of time
once we have felt the universe turn toward us
and have become of it then we too will turn

so many cities have I lived in now and you
and the music of the cars and steam pipes
the violin player praying in the underground
music rising briefly above the subway trains
and harmonizing before the police come through
your lips whispering your thighs warm and close
so many forests I have camped in built cabins
where we could pretend we were wood nymphs
slipping through time with the eyes of animals
once there was a time I thought we would be
well not in this place not upon this street corner
not upon this dark river hidden in mountains
yet in all times and so we are together here lost

in a world of money and war and fear for our children
living wherever the winds have laid us down together,
but once were there meadows and otters and deer
and they will come again in their time after our time
and once were there a time we were together and
in this moment in this space we are now and much
    is good
and all that has been good even among the bad will
be here in its time we share and the time we don't,
and really where words fail me this is all we need.

Just a Fistful of Change

Even though I do have a schedule to keep today
the ink-masters are in for a let-down on the front range.
At seven I'm downstairs for coffee with the News,
at eight the dog takes his walk with me.
At nine I check my emails and investments.
At ten I'm on my way up into the mountains.
At eleven I pull my first fish from the glacier.
At twelve it's time to climb up to the cabin
and look around noting the state of vegetation
now that the ski lift expansion is complete,
noting too the amount of wood still waiting to be cut
will still be the same and the trees sufficient for winter.
At one I take a drive through a virtual ghost town
that has grown up through my memories and
rescue another dog waiting in the road to be taken home
having been abandoned by someone I know I would hate.
At four I'm already cooking dinner for my wife and two dogs
and The Markets have closed The President choked.
The children terrified by their SAT tests at school have
gone home and the mothers and fathers gathered
together in their homes with all the future of our world
and all the future generations that will have to guide us
have gone up to their baths and beds and story-times
and I've gone on to my second or third drink shipped
in from wherever the hell they brew that stuff now, and
I don't suppose anyone will ever pay me for this, and

I don't suppose that anyone should because I am, and we all are down through the years, doing what we can where the mountain wilderness confronts concrete rattling around in an eternal pocketful of change.

Mr. Dick in his First Suit

Dick is going to be a good man someday.
He's got a jackhammer living in his radiators
down near the soup kitchen in the Bowery,
and he's got a troll dying in his refrigerator,
but he's got the symphony of the city in his eyes
twilight cold with the understanding of you
sitting in your silence waiting for light to intrude,
And he's going to bring home the paycheck
each week drawn from fists curled around pads
documenting the shift of money around town
and drawing it toward him before he eats
turning the flowers of Brooklyn into his sweat
and the deer of upstate suburbs to the fat
he draws a belt around each morning rising
to meet the dawn and washing off the day's waste,
He's going to come in that door one day, take
you by the hand and sweep you off your feet
with every intention of honesty he was born of
and offer you all the best of security he knows.
He's got his first suit now and he's on his way.

Dear Microbes With Your March

and with your sacrifice and your glory for the greater
and with your disembowelment on the slopes of irony,
with your passing of the gaseous torch light flaming now
a matchstick held inches from your crotch eliminating odor
and lighting up that which brings us all together, give glory
for we work together as one whatever others believe, and
in our harmony we will preserve the body electric, becoming
one person, a part of one people, surviving where others perish.

We be the gluteous maximus deus machinus that powers
The People driven by the inner sanctum small intestine that powers
the greater cardio pulmonary system and hypocampus extraordinare
fartwaves of energy radiating outward in naked delecte, turn away
your eyes from the man hidden behind the dulcet curtains
and the silks and hardware/software imported improbable, these
are ambiguations of where the chromosomes are going now,
but these Olympics bring us all together where we live as one
in the body electric with a mind of our own formed of multitudes
we move as one upon a journey greater than any we have known.

The Cover of Wings

The cover on the book is never enough.
It is the cover, and poetry the counterpoint
that fills the spaces between the passion and pain…
the trembling vibration that shatters glass in opera halls
echoes dawn in the thunder of besieged cities and souls
the children learning death is the wings of which dreams are made.

In the Community of Trust

There is a community of people
        slow talking men and women
who are blind and deaf to the media
but live in books, classrooms, old folk songs
dating back to a time before our nation
   and before any nation now extant
who watch the stars at night and the rivers
and hold the moon in their crystal goblets;
who build plats laying out our urban streets
and nodes connecting stores and dreams
in the dark green dust of human studies,
whose eyes are almost as bright as yours
and who see that as time passes there is almost
never a need to respond to the crises of time
if we plan ahead there is a circular logic there
is a universe of meanings and other meanings
and facts heaped down upon a table in a hall
where such people come and raise a glass.
I'm glad that we have been among them,
you and I unsettled and unpaid and lost,
and I'm glad that they have forgotten us
and I'm glad that they are there and the world
is as it is with ideas and cultures wrapping round
and finding time and place for each of us who
walk outside the circles and get lost and tossed
beyond anything that has meaning to this time.

Taking What the West Winds Spawn

Lawnmowers roaring their way into autumn sunset
        Clouds   **Scattered**
          but heavy
  in front of the front range mountains of Colorado I
am preparing this evening to drive across the country
      Gold   **Gray Smoke**   **Fire Folded**
with my wife for twenty-three days there and back to say
in poetry what the world is like one election to the next
when men of little mind or words, and those of greater,
have little to say in the face of our continent and world and cosmos
as the seasons shift toward greater violence. Why not men
       Pressing rolling   **Eastward**
of greater violence too…well, I hope not but we do what we do
   what we do
and floods have begun to savage the country like never before
this year in the deep south and along the eastern seaboard where
I am going too through the heartland of wheat fields where
crops grown all year are suddenly wiped out in flash flood where
our breadbasket has been for generations men are hunting where
they will have the best chance to earn a living and survive where
       Taking what the west winds spawn
they can raise their families and maintain their dignity where
the climate has moved into high speed in their shift to violence
where the wild rabbits have eaten off most of the meadow grass
where it has not gotten quite enough to drink and snaps off dry
where you walk on it, and men hunting rabbits and deer and wild

boar or fishing the scattered ponds and rivers that were dry until
the flash floods came to take them away also. Now or in days I
will drive across those miles where the bridges have washed away
and lives have been lost while others have been saved and Blacks
and Latinos have been shot and school children killed this fall
across America I am going to see how many changes there are
in one drive across this country and back in twenty-three days
that I am aware of through my own eyes and the eyes of cameras
          delivering the dust that coats our bones
maintained by our international media, which mostly misses the mist
rising from our fields and the farmers seeding dry mud to dust.

And then at dawn coffee taken in over chipped enamel glaze
tank filled bags packed   dog slipped into car   you can do this too
          see how it all plays out.
     Flowers sedges grasses the color of evening clouds
               but drier and brittle
not the heavy battlewagons carrying water to the great plains.

It is a Strong Wind

It is a strong wind that wraps around my house
tonight rattling the windows shaking oaken walls
tearing at the maple trees that shelter these eaves
now hurling the garbage cans along our alleyway
banging their hard edges along the cement grinding down
throwing old newspapers torn across the landscape.
It is a hard wind that sweeps around us lifting up
and scattering the thoughts of sleep upon eternity,
It is a hard wind that sweeps across our country
slamming against the baked brick walls of factories
swinging the stoplights across small towns like
the brakeman on a freight swinging his lantern
    to light up whatever has passed
in the event that it is coming up upon us as fast as night
and it is a strong wind sweeping across the universe
and it is the same wind sweeping the immense energy
of nova stars and displaced molecules and universes
and here in our minds and in our hearts it is contained
and the windows rattle and the walls break down.
We hold to what we can, sail silver girl.

Is This to Sing

It is when I wake to sing
  your name soft in the spring willows
    of some distant valley where the shadows never fall
death takes me again and again
  in my most wakeful moments if I fall
    and you are not there to hear me do I fall into you
in falling into the earth or do the grasses extend
merely as fire fuses up into the dry roar of sun…
  and there it ends?

Like the Sun Over Primeval Earth

I like to think of sunshine
coming over the mountains
and filling each green fiber that grows
with the distance of uncounted miles,
but justice starts before that because
of the lives that settle into the silt of oceans
and the so slow grinding of continental drift
and the seeds that were planted millennia ago,
the earth rolling over into itself, rising upward
toward where the air is more thin and pure
and those seeds begin then to branch out as lichen
and moss springs at last from almost lifeless rock peaks
so that after time has been forgotten, gone unmeasured,
those soft and vulnerable green tendrils begin to reach
that sun

that came from beyond memory and beyond meaning.
Like this, I think of genetic memory beyond time
and of the seeds of human misunderstanding reaching out
and trying to carry human growth one more step beyond
this pitiful bag of rags we carry on our bone. We try,
but in the flash of a lifetime captured on media, most
things are done too fast, and what is fast is mostly wrong
and is buried in the arms of nations turned against each other.
I know it is the little things unnoticed that go on,

that get passed from one generation to another, one
Harriet Tubman, one Martin Luther King, one Kennedy,
one Gandhi, one starving boy not exposed to media but
stretched out upon the mountains, draped beneath the cosmos,
cold and dying but reaching out toward that greater source
of life, that sun that breathes life into our souls across darkness
that makes a difference across the raft of generations, that
builds justice beyond the understanding of tired men
and is justice that brings peace to those we never know.

In a Street Café

Two aging men are drinking coffee
and one asks the other what it has come down to
and the other talks of money and children and one job or another
and the other talks about poetry without giving it name or stanzas
and each one of them nods forcefully and dabs his lips with a napkin
without either one knowing what words should come next and
neither one of them has anything left to take home but words
and neither one is particularly sad at this or feels lost
having shared a bit of life together and someone
else is brewing a bitter drink, but not they.

The Tombstones That are Tuning Forks

Floyd was a silhouette against Phoenix that evening
and the stars peppered the darkness that surrounded him
as he talked of the old days, his words passages in wind
closing a loop that we all were entered into and yet cut short.
There was a dignity born of lost dreams and forgotten love
and yet also a distance spoken of by coyotes beyond him in the hills
so that their voices and his wavered across a chronometric scale
while the desert burned on side of us and the city ate our souls.

That's how I remember him…a shadow pasted against the night
singing a song with his words that I could not understand but
which brought the earth to life around him and enlightened him,
an old man who had once sold homes, birthed children, hated
the clocks that ruled his life, and warned us of those thigs that night
as he turned his soul toward the bottle he raised in our honor, he
chose his words as carefully as he ever had because they filled that night
and their meaning still just half formed by his brain and the alcohol
distilling it and wearing down his flesh, pitting confusion in his soul
somehow in that magic moment found its up-swelling and meaning
in his heart, in his being, in his lungs, and burst upon his throat
finding a long-drawn meaning beyond words which beat upon his lips,
filtered through his teeth, caught against the loose flesh of his throat
and echoed out the meaning of what it was to be a man to be a Floyd,
to be adrift, and what is left now years later when he is in a box
tongue gone words lost night ended and the teeth but tombstones,
    tuning forks that know the night of eternity.

When the Storm Came Upon Us

The skies were opened by wind last night.
Stars swept down and battered bedroom walls.
Mortgages shifted their dry husks in drawers.
Families talked in their dreams with the departed.
Nothing to fear in all the vast spaces above us,
we were left to spread our arms and sail beyond.

The Light is Different

The light itself is different
the way it comes from stars.
Dust becomes it.
Life is hardier, galloping
on cloven hooves.
Men smell of sage brush
or of aspen, not old desks,
coming in from the range.
The pines taller, sand deeper
rocks sharper, alleys canyons.
Whatever happens in life
happens with most immediacy
snugged against the western sun.

Each Crystal Different and the Same

The first snow flake had dead flesh at its core
whirled high above the streets and factories and continents
and ice cased that flesh and swirled down upon a continent
appearing as a fragile, crystal prism nestled on the ground
And it was the first of many, and one after another
each as different from the other as your DNA from another
they began to form around dark soot and flesh and bone
and they drifted down with a starved child at their core
or the end life of a coal miner from the hills of Virginia
or the drops of oil spilled from cross country pipelines
or a mother's child grown too old upon the streets and cold
they settled one upon another, and at their heart, the heart
within each one of the heart of the human race caught up
and lifted up, torn away into the sky to dance down
in a cold and sterile blanket indifferent to mankind.

What a Sunset It Is!

What a sunset we have this evening,
the end of the week, no deadlines to meet,
no reason to answer the telephone or texts
and the lawn extends to the distant mountains
carved in cardboard against the evening…
a glass of scotch, a dram of wine, and you
spread out against the breeze of evening.

How much longer we would have lived
if we had known each evening was as this,
how much less the pressure in our veins,
the adrenaline tearing away our innocence
the anger directed at those who are now gone.
But it's okay, because the sun sets silently
and star upon star comes into being while we watch
and that's enough, much more than enough
as the miles between us expand across this plain
and we are together outlaws in love, this evening
the sunset sets across all those mountains we live among.

An Evening in September

My dog has been waiting outside for me
for half an hour before I grab a brandy and go to join him
to watch The Big Dipper set into its forever place
and listen to the crickets of September making love,
and yet he huddles up against me and I press his side to my leg
wondering in all this space why we cannot name each star
or why I cannot name the animals that scent the wind
as he does as we expand ourselves into the cosmos.
His molecules and mine becoming one where words fail
and our protons interacting on a subatomic scale
where emotion and understanding of the animal take place.
We have a peace in this, an understanding beyond species
and life to life across eternity is as peaceful as life allows.

Friends and Lovers

For twenty years I lived
in the house of my parents
and read their books
and drank their wine.
For forty years now I
fashioned my house
in the blueprints of theirs.
Only recently have I begun
to open the old closet doors
open the drawers of bureaus
unopened for sixty years,
and find them empty, waiting
for something new to fill them,
knowing that was my job, not
earning the same coins over again.
Not lying in those closed boxes
with all my friends and lovers.

Guitar Plucked Note by Note

brandy before candlelight
breathing the foundations of furnishings
off curved glass walls   flames
   licking her swan curved neck
  the worn walnut bench in the corner amber
snow snapping the screens outside

I come unfocussed
my mind like the liquor
with flames of resonant intensity
curving in upon each other and
gone before illumination

the memories of what we are
stored in old wooden boxes
haunting darkened rooms
perfume bottles unopened
coated with years of dust
    a guitar plucked note by note
no song to sing not yet despite the chorus.

A Gathering of Ghosts

        We speak when the fireplace roars
dead toppled aspen trees on this mountain
                smoke billowing
caught between the room we sit in
      and the chimney heavy choking
  branches burning in the trees of night.
Old logs harvested eighty years ago
  encapsulating my wife's family
I am a willing guest and progenitor of ghosts
here in this cabin her father, grandfather,
                uncles and aunts built
in the wilderness of the grid
                    oh! these mountains!
where the wind blows over their bones
  between these peaks where elk graze
       the mountain lions, bears
              otters in morning brooks
so light in the morning, but here we are
with the night outside and these generations!
I have a scotch deep in this wilderness
        where I find peace
          and speak
to my wife as we each read our separate books
like a cat coiling around our lungs
she listens to the little girl of magic

        she was and will
              always be
among these family members buried on this mountain
and answers among the ghost
        I find myself alone
            at peace
                alone
in this dowry you wife were bequeathed
What do you hear! What do you hear!
        And what am I ghosting in this space?

In Wilderness There is no Virtue

for Henry David Thoreau

When you are among the trees there is no virtue, Henry.
The bones of the mountains are wrapped around you,
and the sky so open, the alpine rivulets pure as cold crystal,
you are a long way from the dirt choked streets of impotence,
from the gold crusted maple polished desks of indifference
with which this country now powers itself. Indeed in which all
men have slaved against each other giving despair and death.

Oh, I know that you raised enough to eat on a rich man's land,
and lived there picking arrowheads from the soil for one year
while you tried to forget the pencils you have packed in boxes.
I have noted the changing of the seasons, as did you, listed
the coming and going of flowers and little creatures and songs,
and some of them were in concrete alleys and others in fields.
That's how I know it is not so simple and we got it wrong.
I wish my publisher too walked the greens of Boston Commons
with the transcendent eye we know so well, but I too would fail
because the eye alone is not transcendent and that city is far
from this strange strip of rocky forest on the nation's spine.

I hold one green shoot in my hand and look out over the cliff
that lies between me and the valley below and city below that
which is but a faint white tower edged below the horizon, and
there are miles of trees and brush and moose and elk between

and fish in the streams and I am living loose and simple, but
I cannot and will not forget or disavow the men and women
I worked with for less than minimum wage or the factories
or the evening streets I sold encyclopedias door to door along
or the woman in a Hyatt Hotel who plunged to her death
cascading through the atrium where I held a business meeting
or how a human body gives a little away each day it is alone,
and we spend so many days alone even in our concrete shells.
No there is no virtue here in nature as it is today, just another way
to stay alive in a time we all choose our own enclosures.

Having Lived With the Muse for 50 Years

The tide is going out,
starfish and sea urchins caught in tidal pools
that drain away into mudflats beneath a cold sun.
I am farther away than I have ever meant to be.
The salt air has turned to desert, the wild storms all
but forgotten in this technological land above the waves,
but I am reminded at times like these there are eyes
looking up from the bottom of the bay two thousand miles
away from where I have wandered that do not know of me
or dream that there are demons above them a continent away
who will come searching among the skeletons of those they eat
as I will some day still if I live that long and if they do,
and their eyes are looking up all this time from the mud
not the slightest bit aware of the metal hooks that guide us all,
the metal hooks that bring us out for one last flash against the sun.

I hope to go there one last time
when the warning flags are flying, waves strong at my back
one last time to be aware of the egrets standing in the marshes,
the terns turning about me, the ocean reaching in
to press around my thighs as I stand upon the shore of time
casting a line out as thin as spider web and twice as strong
to catch the mysteries of another hidden universe.

Outside Caribou

The weathered boards of his abandoned farmhouse caught evening in the grain of their wood and smoothed it out across fields populated by last autumn's harvest and this spring's Indian grasses and a wind that blew the miles from west to east and the shadows that seemed to weave them all together so that you had to squint, to really focus your eyes on the here and now to even see it at all as it sat there growing slowly back into the scenery, the doors open so that they too filled themselves with a lack of shape or purpose, though when I went inside the air still held the scent of old flesh and all the rooms were furnished with what a family might want in a worse time…a simple plank table rough hewn in the kitchen and a single shelf over the window with a cracked ceramic bowl, an empty refrigerator lying open and unplugged, some plugs of dust leading into the sitting room empty but for an overstuffed sofa, and the empty stairway leading up to what I'm sure were empty beds.

She wasn't there anymore either, nor her family, just an unplugged radio without much purpose anymore now that the land was drying out, and had made clear as dust its intentions to take the farm back again. Not a minor thing, because their hands had planted seeds that lived their lives each year in the acreage that surrounded them, had felt the sun each day and the cold rains and been culled and harvested generation after generation through his hands and his sons', but the land and the elements we work with live forever and we do not.

Tributaries

The Colorado where it arises among tall grasses
springing from sands beneath the Never Summer Mountains
with all the wily trout that twist among its roots
and the gold metal glint that catches each rising sun
with the spring melt swelling it is only a tributary
as it leaves the western edge of Estes Park flowing south

and when it is heaving its turgid way through Arizona
cleaving the massive cliffs that lie above it the markers
the Ancient Ones laid down now half erased by sun still
scattering the bones of its first Caucasian explorers out
cataloging the land in tumult but a minor tributary still
in its downward southward flooding of man's mystery

and when it slowly trickles to its last south of our border
leaving only oiled foul smelling stains after the hardest rains
and then a dry valley which once filled the land with birds
and fish and flowed forever into the largest ocean we have
it is, like you, but a tributary each vessel each artery you carry
filling each limb each taste of life each neuron in each hand
building a fulfilling understanding of our time and land and place.

Fishing Below Timberline

This time I lay the line out long and smooth
and it stretches like silk along the waters and above the stones
and its reflection is caught within the clouds and between the
    creatures
that are never seen within their native habitat and are hidden
    from ours,
and the line lies there lightly curled beneath the sunshine and dips slowly
where it flows into the deep dark pools where life hides itself so softly
it is wind whispering from my hands to the earth whispering
    across water.

Something connects and the line is drawn farther,
unspools itself into the mystery that no man can see from where
    I stand
my boot heels scrabbling into the shoreline rubble and sand sifting
    into time
and my weight being too much for the lightness that fills this
    afternoon.
A hawk sails above me, and I know that a line floats gossamer
    between us,
and my heart soars on dark feathers that have no home known to man.
The water is cold beneath these mountains and the sun hot
dancing off their surface and life commands itself,
this time as I set the hook smooth and wait.

Here in the West

So many things out here can kill you instantly
   (aside from men and cars)
        the cougar in evening
   those things that haunt the shadows
the snakes
   the winds that tear off roofs
     the cold that shatters stars,
that only here you can really come to life:
that is why the air is clearest
        the sunsets from the mouths of volcanos
   colors that Georgia O'Keefe could almost capture
along the backbone of a continent
where machines migrate with the antelope

That Time of Year the West is Best Defined

That time of year,
a leathering after the sun has beaten down
and the high grasses have turned to straw
been flattened by the months of drought
and sand has begun to spread among their roots

That time of year,
the oil roustabouts head out to check their rigs
when the winds sharpen color in the landscape
and rock again claims the shapes of mountains,
when snakes coil into their autumn dens
the flesh of men gets sand blasted along all
these miles and cultures and generations all
along these western miles of settlements on edge

That time of year,
women gather in the shopping malls while
spirits of Hopis, Navaho, Apaches, Arapahos, Cheyenne,
Utes storm against the windows of Mexicans and Anglos,
getting ground against their skin and souls engrained pressed
and swept across the immense majesty of minds
raging back and forth in the winds of the Chinooks
that light fire to these mountain ranges of mankind

That time of year,
when man comes together in the dry wilderness
having moved one more year toward retirement from his office
looking for survival in the adobe walls and wooden bridges
native to this part of the country where the roads run out
and every man now has to find himself, his soul
between all the diverse media and cultures
which all men strive to strike from stone
from the frozen fields of Montana to the kiln of Arizona
and all our cities encampments farms and empty trails

That time of year which is native to this land alone
that spawns the storms and riches that feed us
and sweeps across all of those who sleep beyond.
That time of year where the West is best defined.

Hollow Seeds Inside the Space You Left

Wind blowing makes the house do unusual things
after a long night of drinking the walls seem to move
and dust rises out of the front range to darken the sun
so that when I hung on the front door jamb my coffee
cup curled in one gnarled hand thinking I heard her
horse coming back into the lower paddock this morning
and saw only the earth moving with the speed of wind
I wondered half asleep whoever built this home anyway
and why would I still think of her here among sagebrush
and dry things that blow away, but this morning that is
what I did, and the windows rattled, my own horse
Juanita shifted in her stall and called to the wild stallion
that last came through these parts at least a decade ago.

Everything poised for something unknown to happen
in this little plot of land where life was getting harder
and the dust was all I had to talk to as the mind woke
and I looked out toward the horizon over arid peaks
and thought I saw well maybe it was just a dust devil
coiled around the bright emergence of sun from cloud
but that morning the ground shook like never before
and the winds of time tore through me I swear I felt
connections to dreams that had no place in time, and
there was a column of fire upon the mountains rising
miles into the sky and I was blinded and the birds
fell into silence and the air glowed and I thought
of gods and devils that dance in the Superstitions

and of Spanish gold and the Lost Dutchman
coming back to search for it and pirate ships
crossing the dark void we had come from
thundering in another time and space
and I cried but nothing happened in that place,
not in that time not far northwest of Santa Fe.

At the End

We leave nothing here.
So cold tonight I swear
the windows will shatter
in my house, blue shards
of birds piercing my flesh
and the winds will hollow
as heartbeats on caskets.

So Like the Metal Cattle Cars

I don't know what the kill mechanism is
hidden under the football helmets and padding
and in gun cabinets across family rooms,
but the man downstairs went into his den
last night with his dog thinking doggie thoughts
and his wife outside and closed the door
and put a bullet through his head,

and he won't ever have to worry about healthcare
or Medicare Part B or his daughter's education
or whether the country is great again or not,
or how the universe fell away from his wife
who will lie awake in horror the rest of her life
or remember why he bought that damned tube
of metal so like the metal cattle cars he rode.

Beyond the Heavy, Slow Machinery

The sod houses have vanished from these plains.
They have turned into the roads that dot our hills
and have blown away into sunrise that blinds beginnings.
In the north men build their homes of ice, not stone
but the essence of what fills their veins.

Now the majority sterile as hospitals in white gowns, Auntie
Septic fills our nostrils as we hunt for what grows slow.
Trees covered with paint take a long time to grow
and are further removed from us than mud and straw
slapped together with the lime from old bones. Not
human weather chimes but the frames of small sea creatures
left out in the desert sun too long so long ago they are sand.

Shattered desert glass bottles gather atop these walls,
the skeletons of adobe forts holding back time and progress.
People gather like crows and begin to chant shadows.
Wind listens and has little to say of where we came from.
Distance so vast.

Music that obliterates the heavy, slow machinery we knew,
the earth closer to our skin.

This is the American Dream, and What of Joe

Big Joe hauls the groceries in
from the backseat of a beat-up Dodge each week
with never one sick week in his life, but
he sits at a desk six days of seven turning numbers
forty years after Romantic Poetry at Harvard
and teaching Linguistics at Charlotte and UIC
and he remembers the phyla of each green flower
he sees in his memory as he walks the fields
in memory it is getting harder to breathe and
he stops to catch his breath again and again
with each week he is immortal until he dies.

This is the American Dream,
and where are all the professors?
What magic do they breathe into their lungs
where capitalism fills the desert canyons.
Surely it is something potent, powerful,
and invisible as the oxygen that fills our lungs
and the starlight that fills the night lights their pipes.
This is the American Dream, and what of Big Joe
and all his studies, degrees and hours now gone.

Jared Smith is the author of 14 books of poetry, 2 CDs, and stage productions in New York and Chicago. He has served on the Editorial Boards of *Home Planet News, The New York Quarterly, Turtle Island Quarterly*, and *The Pedestal Magazine,* as well as on the Board of Directors of literary and arts non-profits in New York, Illinois, and Colorado. Jared has taught at New York University, La Guardia Community College, and Illinois Institute of Technology. He has also worked as Vice President of a consulting company, Associate Director of Education and Applied Technology Research at Institute of Gas Technology; Special Advisor to Argonne National Laboratory; and as a technical advisor to The White House under President Clinton. He lives in Colorado, where he spends much of his time in a rustic log cabin in Roosevelt National Forest.

www.ingramcontent.com/pod-product-compliance
Lightning Source LLC
Chambersburg PA
CBHW020124130526
44591CB00032B/512